SALINE DISTRICT LIBRARY

D1034980

WITHDRAWN

Voelker's Pond

Voelker's Pond

A ROBERT TRAVER LEGACY

By *photographer* ED WARGIN

With essays by JAMES MCCULLOUGH

SALINE DISTRICT LIBRARY
555 N. Maple Road
Saline, MI 48176

Huron River Press ~ Chelsea, Michigan

Text copyright © James McCullough
Photographs copyright © Ed Wargin

All rights reserved. No part of this book may be reproduced in any manner
without the express written consent of the publisher, except in the case of brief
excerpts in critical reviews and articles. All inquiries should be addressed to:

Clock Tower Press, LLC
320 North Main Street
P.O. Box 310
Chelsea, MI 48118
www.clocktowerpress.com
Huron River Press is an imprint of Clock Tower Press.

Printed and bound in Canada.

10 9 8 7 6 5 4 3 2 1

Library of Congress Cataloging-in-Publication Data
Wargin, Ed.
  Voelker's pond : a Robert Traver legacy / by photographer, Ed Wargin ;
with essays by James McCullough.
     p. cm.
  ISBN 1-932399-00-3
  1. Trout fishing–Michigan–Upper Peninsula–Anecdotes. 2. Voelker,
John D. (John Donaldson), 1903—Anecdotes. I. McCullough, James, 1961- II.
Title.
  SH688.U6W366 2003
  799.1'757'097749--dc21
                              2003004718

To order fine art gallery prints of the images contained in this book, please
contact the photographer at 1-866-526-0998 or 1-231-348-7094. He may
also be reached through his website at www.thewargincompany.com or via
email at ew@edwargin.com.

To John D. Voelker, rest his soul, for his enduring writings and example, and, to Voelker's Pond, a personality of its own, for calling us back time and again, may you stay healthy and wild forever.

Photographer's Note

Every time I press a camera to my face, I am
given the chance to see the world in a new way,
and for that I feel fortunate.

I have worked around the world, yet am always
amazed at the beauty of our own backyards.
Voelker's Pond exemplifies that beauty. The
physical area in which James McCullough and
I worked was quite small, but its imprint was
enormous. As we worked, the project became
an exercise in seeing the obvious as well as the
not so obvious.

I am excited to share this world with you, and
I hope that seeing the images of Voelker's Pond
inspires us all to think about slowing down
the pace of our lives, if only a little. For
when we do, the mundane details of everyday life become not so mundane, and not so
everyday.

I believe that we all have a Voelker's Pond in
our life—some back country, quiet repose,
gentle innocent place—there to shape our life
if we let it. So, please enjoy this journey to
Voelker's Pond, and may it show you the road
to the places you love best.

ED WARGIN

Preface

We have preserved in words and images what we could of Voelker's pond, as a record for posterity, to hold the moments still, long enough for us to enjoy, to share, to imagine, so we might return to them again and again to see what they might teach us.

"Old fishermen never die," Voelker wrote "instead they write books about their passion, usually couched in a mournful, elegiac, Thoreauesque prose." Perhaps they are elegiac, but we hope these images and words inspire as well. Admittedly, at times I am like those outdoorsmen who at one time or another must imagine they were born into the wrong decade or century, or at least cannot help, no matter their circumstances, but fantasize about the days gone by and how much better it must have been, or even, how much better it must be elsewhere. And thinking like this, we come one way or another to see that most modern reflection, like most modern art, is about loss. Our childlike days are behind us; the great leaders, gone; the story once told can never be new again. Our words, as former poet laureate Robert Hass tells us, are "elegy to what they signify." That is, our words will always give tribute to what is past, what is no longer. For fishermen, the fish, if kept, can never be caught again; if released, can never be caught again for the first time. The lesson John Voelker might pass on to us, then, is to keep on fishing and telling yarns about your day.

There are reservations in writing a book like this, since calling attention to beautiful places often, and ironically, rings a death knell for them. I hope, with all due respect, that these images are enough, and that no one having read this book tries to find Frenchman's uninvited. Instead, I'd have us all consider this: Until John Voelker came to love his pond, it was an out-of-the-way backwater in a remote region of a rugged land. But it was in his homeland, his "bailiwick." He found the beauty there, loved it, and brought it to our eyes. So, while one lesson of Voelker's pond is that there is no place like it, another is that there are millions more just as moving, just as magical.

Contents

*John Voelker's original
Trout Unlimited
membership card.*

Introduction

I met John Voelker 26 years ago, near the
end of a trip that began when my father and I
loaded his Scout II with fly casting and camping
gear and began a weeklong expedition north
from our home in Petoskey across the Straits of
Mackinac through the Upper Peninsula, west,
along the route Hemingway's character Nick
Adams takes by train to Seney, Michigan, in
the famous short story, *Big Two Hearted River*.
In the story, Nick hikes past the town and the
burned-out landscape into the lush countryside
to recover from an unspoken wound, and catches
trout with every cast using live grasshoppers
he'd caught in the cool of the morning, until he
hooks, battles, and snaps off the big one at the
brim of a swamp, a dangerous swamp he would
have to leave for another time. We, however,
drove on a dusty road, got sunburned in August
heat, fished all day while getting peppered by
deerflies, and caught nothing. Later on in the
trip we fished the Two Hearted, and other
streams, but my father's final destination, and
the true reason for the pilgrimage, lay farther
north, past the territory where Hemingway
traveled in life, past where Nick Adams travels
in fiction, beyond the great boggy flats to the
rugged, glacier-worn northern rim of the Upper
Peninsula, the land we call Traver Country.
There we would meet and fish with John Voelker.

To avid readers of 1950s best-sellers and
to classic film buffs, Robert Traver, the author,
may need no introduction, but others may not
know his real name, John Voelker, the man
Charles Kuralt befriended after profiling him
for his *On the Road* series, and who in the end
Kuralt said was "the closest thing to a great
man [he] ever met."

*From Charles Kuralt's visit to
the pond during filming of his
"On the Road" television series.*

If you haven't read John Voelker's essays, you may never hear so eloquently how true fishermen enter the world of trout, and why a person ought to do so. There is no machismo or conquest with Voelker. There are few considerations of size and weight, relative to fish or fly. He does not tell where to fish or how to get there or where to stay. What you'll find is a fair amount of self-deprecating humor, deft descriptions of flubbed-up casts and other failures turned to happiness, so that losing a fly while balancing through a bog leads to meeting a friend on the other side. For Voelker, fishing is a joyous pursuit full of humor, humility, and friendships, and other ingredients necessary for approaching "trout wisdom."

Born a bartender's son in 1903 in Ishpeming, on the northern rim of Michigan's Upper Peninsula, Voelker somehow made his way from this most remote and distant region of the state, 500 or so miles south to Ann Arbor where at first he nearly flunked out, then in the end earned his way to a University of Michigan law degree. There he met and afterward married Grace Taylor from Oak Park, Hemingway's hometown, and took a position with a large firm in Chicago. But he could not stand the oppressive, entry-level job or urban life, and soon returned to the U.P. where he was elected district attorney, and where he began writing under the name Robert Traver. Later on, he was elevated to the Michigan Supreme Court before leaping to fame with the success of his best seller, *Anatomy of a Murder*, a novel that soon after was turned into an Academy Award winning film directed by Otto Preminger and starring Jimmy Stewart, Lee Remick, and George C. Scott.

Impressive as they are, his political, legal, and artistic successes did not immortalize Voelker in the world of fly-fishing; rather, he was immortalized by his willingness to abandon them. At the height of his power, of fame as an author and of influence in the highest court in Michigan, he chose to "flee the baying hounds of success" by stepping down, returning to his simple home in the rugged Upper Peninsula and devoting the rest of his life to his passions: fishing from spring to fall and writing about fishing all winter, a routine that produced such classics as *Trout Madness*, *Anatomy of a Fisherman*, and *Trout Magic*.

He became ritualistic—more and more, it seems, as the years went on, picking up his mail in the mornings, meeting friends at the Rainbow Bar in Ishpeming, driving over 20 miles of dirt road to avoid one mile of pavement on his way to fish camp, fishing until the five o'clock cabin break for cocktails and cribbage. But all the while, in mind and in motion, alone or with his closest friends, he pursued the shy, native brook trout that haunt the vast waterways of the

Escanaba River basin, and especially—particu-
larly—the "mermaids" in a remote stretch of
spring-fed water he owned, where my father
and I would join him.

At times he and his friends called the place
"Frenchman's Creek" ("for that is not its name,"
he wrote) or "Frenchman's," "Frenchman's
Pond," "Uncle Tom's," "Uncle's" or "fish camp,"
and he wrote lovingly of its inhabitants' feminine
dispositions. He could catch trout there only
when they were, as he put it, "in the mood."

Learning to fly-fish with me was one of my
father's most profound gifts, more than he may
know, but equally, so was this pilgrimage to
meet a man who had achieved the heights of
success and was willing to chuck all social
expectation with a confident grin, who was
unafraid to live on his own terms, and who
chose to spend his time simply and humbly,
among friends, fishing the vast waterways in
the landscape that he loved. ～

The drive leading
into the cabin.

The Road In

We met him in the parking lot, shook hands, and he smiled right away, calling me "Shamus" though that is not my name, and I liked him immediately. Tall with big hands and a weathered, happy face, he was dressed in khaki pants and shirt with a cigar sticking out of the pocket, worn leather boots and a round, weather-worn hat with a small brim. "Well," he said then, and turned to his fish car. My father and I piled into our Scout and followed him out of town at ten miles under the speed limit and slower still when we hit dirt roads, then down to a trot on the two-tracks, snailing along for miles, watching the back of his white Jeep, brake lights on more than off. I still remember the tension between my desire to show respect and my adolescent need to get somewhere. Finally frustrated enough with his opossum's pace I said, "Where's he going?" I was certain we'd turned at one time or another to every point on the compass. I looked to my father, who shrugged.

Then he stopped. I thought finally we had arrived at a trail to a fishing hole, but his door did not open. Instead, an arm extended out of his window, then a finger pointed at something on the ground that we could not make out until we pulled ahead and craned our necks to see a nest of white orchids, delicate, cupped like children's hands, nearly hidden by undergrowth a foot or two off the beaten track. We admired them as he got out with a pair of snippers and clipped one.

There was a pause, then my dad asked, "Aren't those protected?"

"Well," he said, "from time to time I have to bend the statute, sir," and he placed the flower in a bucket of water, then hopped back in the Jeep.

An old minstrel decorates the outside of the cabin.

Ten minutes later he came to a complete stop again and without a word or glance toward us, he reached into the back of his fish car, retrieved a white plastic bucket, turned and sauntered into the woods. We piled out and waited, wondering what he was up to until he returned with a pair of white shelf-fungus. He said they were edible and grew on dead aspen, but they looked like old boot toes to me, and now I suspect the harvest was part theater, but I was quick to want to please the master. As we started up again, I searched above the scrub pines for the tops of poplars and within 50 yards, deep in the brush I spied the top of a thick, dead aspen and, tracing down toward its trunk, spotted a mound of mushrooms. I marked the tree and called out, "Stop!", frightening my father, and I leaped out through the brambles, returning with my arms heavy with musty mushrooms. I handed them over to Mr. Voelker, who thanked me, a bit undone I think by my performance. "How did you see those?" my father asked, and I beamed the rest of the way in.

A little later, the judge repeated the orchid trick with his clippers and some wild roses.

After an hour or more of four-wheel sauntering, our attention spans sputtering, we followed him off a sandy road onto a lesser worn dirt two-track that descended through second growth pines and over an enormous glacial rock that required slow going, tilting us sideways, then dropping us down a gully and through a small, muddy stream, then up again into some tall birch and aspen and into a tight canopy of maples, where we read a hand-painted sign, "Warning: Bridge Out." A few old fenders, mufflers, and car parts were strewn about there, by way of discouraging the uninvited. We followed, until we came to a thick cable across the road, locked down with an old German key lock the size of a woodcutter's fist. He dropped the cable and waved us on, past another sign that read brazenly, "Home of the Upper Peninsula Cribbage Champion," then through an ancient stand of red pines canopied above us, the car having to bump and weave around enormous trunks on a soft matting of needles and over roots round as my thighs. We soon emerged to a sandier section and a more open, flat plain with aspen and bracken fern, some No Trespassing signs. Then suddenly, from where I was sitting, his Jeep appeared to fall headlong into a hole.

The road dropped out from under us also,
so steeply that I had to put my hand on the
dashboard, but in seconds we were stopped
on a flat, gray glacial rock. I stepped out and
stretched. On my left, a rough-hewn cabin not
much longer than our car, a picnic table, and
oddities like horseshoes and telephone insulators, a pair of wooden minstrels. On my right,
the sloping rock and lichen path down to the
dark water of Frenchman's pond. ∼

Various signs adorn the old
parking spot in the woods.

An old bourbon cup engraved
for John with the words,
"In Cabin Still Veritas."

"*Kids have only one Christmas to look forward to each
year, but a fisherman has the same thrill of anticipation
every time he takes off fishing.*" — JOHN VOELKER

A dry fly awaits a visit from
a hungry brook trout.

The Pond

Frenchman's is an ice-cold backwater created by
a series of active beaver dams that have stood
for well over 50 years, maybe 100. Its water is
relatively shallow and seeps up from a mosquito-
rich cedar swamp, filtered clean through deep,
easily disturbed silt beds that rest on glacier-
raked bedrock, billions of years old. The sur-
rounding landscape was formed by the final
recession, ten thousand years ago, of an ice field
so thick and vast it shaped the entire Midwest,
depositing sand and rich soils in vast moraines,
carving out the Great Lakes and leaving behind
the largest source of freshwater in the world,
Lake Superior, only a few miles north.

From deep in bedrock, water seeps up in
springs where trout congregate in the evening
and early morning, and on most overcast days.
Otherwise they seek the cover of fallen trees,
sunken casting stations, weed beds, and undercut banks. But then again, they may decide to
feed actively in shallow water on a sunny day,
against all sense, or hide for days, leaving fishermen to believe the water is barren.

Voelker called it Frenchman's "for that
is not its name." Like all great fishermen, he
would never kiss and tell on a trout stream, but
neither could he have predicted how rapidly the
outside world would expand into his
own. In the late '50s, when he began
writing about the pond, the Upper
Peninsula was only accessible from the Lower
Peninsula by ferry. It wasn't until the comple-
tion of the Mackinac bridge, the "fatal artery,"
that allowed down-staters to travel at highway
speeds into Traver Country.

When I visited in the mid 1970s his cabin
was remote, but I doubt he could have imagined
then how quickly the world would impinge.
I wonder if he would have named it at all.
Still, Frenchman's never was and never will
be open for business.

Its beauty is moody, often muted, mercurial, and intimate, and it defies definition: at high water, it is a creek with a pond's vegetation and a tedious but distinct current. At low water, it is a still, cold-water pond more difficult to fish, more confined. It requires you to slow down, to settle into its own rhythms, yet it makes no promises, except that you earn your keep; it does not impress itself upon you with raging currents or wide sweeping bends, but lulls you into noticing the smallest, most remarkable things: a spider's web, a ringlet of water, a cedar waxwing feeding on something too small for you to see.

Walking the shoreline of Frenchman's Pond is like balancing across a floating field of trap-doors. The ground is pitted and knolled with old stumps hidden in the grass, and clumped with roots, and troughed by ancient beaver runs, and pocked by muskrat holes. There are low, dark inlets that might provide you hard ground to stand on, or you might be in muck three feet deep. Sometimes you set a foot down certain it will hold you, only to find what looked like grass was a vegetable veneer. As you cast,

here and there, a lone branch from a low shrub tricks you and snaps off your fly, or restricts you to roll-casts that rarely, and at best barely stretch far enough to reach the few rising trout you see.

You might circumnavigate the entire pond only to find the vibration of your bumbling footwork has sent the trout down or driven them back to the other side. Or it could be that whatever invisible insect they have keyed in on has stopped hatching where you are, and started where they are. Once, while the rest of the pond remained glassy and still, I witnessed a hatch and feeding fish in an area maybe ten feet in diameter, and nowhere else on the entire pond, a column of mayflies performing their vertical dance, fluttering up, floating down, fluttering up again above the concentric, liquid ringlets of feeding trout, and all of this beyond the reach of my longest cast.

Wading across is impossible, and wading in general is dangerous, since stepping past the bank might mean oozing waist deep into jet-black, boot-sucking muck. Either way, stuck or not, the richest silt releases methane bubbles that percolate up your legs in a witches' stench, leaving you relieved you don't smoke, and certain that even if you somehow survive, a week's worth of tomato baths may not gain you acceptance again in the civilized world. And yet, I wade now and again, probing, prodding, negotiating my own way through. ⌣

"Fishing is essentially a solitary art, usually practiced out of sight and hearing of one's companions…" — J.V.

The Cabin

He could have hired architects to erect a monumental home on some western river, or on a high bank over the Escanaba or Lake Superior, but instead he and his friends found the only solid, flat slab of ground on Frenchman's and built a cedar and pine cabin, shaped like a miniature barn, barely big enough for four people, cramped with five, tucked between the hemlocks at the bottom of a steep bank, only a stone's throw from the pond.

Outside they built a brick stove, a table opposite the cabin door, a storage shed and a rail fence leading to the privy, a sign marking the way, warning: "Bare Area." They never bothered to build walls or a roof, just a plywood box with a hole under a toilet seat and an empty coffee can for the paper. There is no running water or electricity at Frenchman's.

Beside the cabin, they chained a cooler to a tree behind an old picnic table, and over the years added knickknacks and oddities to the trees and shelves along the cabin: license plates and wood-carved minstrels, old glass insulators from telephone poles, a thermometer and such.

Facing the cabin, an old bell still hangs above the door. I have never pulled its rope, but imagine its tone echoing down the pond to ring in the fishermen for four o'clock cocktails, the fishing reports, and friendly wagering.

Inside, the cabin is three paces wide and six deep with sliding glass windows on three sides and a woodstove on the fourth. Memorabilia adorn most shelves and wall space, harkening themes from the old man's writings, his life and works. Tacked to the wall: an old advertisement for Griffin reels with the image of a curvaceous mermaid, taunting, "You'll never catch me without a Griffin Reel"; an original cover of *Trout Magic*; a republished cover of *Trout Madness*; a faded copy of his "Testament to a Fisherman." Also, the echoes of male yearnings: an oil painting of a woman, naked from the waist up, postcards, one from France of two

nudes in soft light, and on a shelf, a glass that reads, CAUTION: CONTENTS OF THIS GLASS MAY LEAD TO INTERCOURSE. Handwritten and painted greeting cards, faded photos of friends and high up, a line of spent bourbon bottles. The cribbage board, candles and cards rest on a custom table with drink shelves built onto the legs. Along the south wall, farthest from the pond, an old green couch that folds out to a bed (though I didn't discover this until this year).

For years I held a reverence for the memorabilia inside the cabin, and snooped, but to find a spoon or a match. But this year as his family began cleaning and rearranging the cabin, I confess I snooped one night after fishing, alone. There is a hanging shelf above with blankets and a comforter I'd donated years before. I was taking the blanket down when I noticed a box full of heavy papers that with a glance I found were maps.

My father and I used to keep plat maps of all the counties where we hunted and fished, so we could study the boundaries between state and private land. We always noted the good grouse hunting or the access roads to rivers. A skull and crossbones where the going is too

rough, an exclamation point, or the number of grouse flushes. I thought, could it be that I have found the fountain of knowledge from the high priest of secrecy, the master woodsman who vowed never to kiss and tell on a trout stream? I pulled down the box to find over 20 maps of Baraga and Marquette counties and flipped through them one by one like mad, searching for a single mark, a green pen, a comment in the margins, anything to indicate success or failure.

What I found were the glossy pages of pristine maps, and the truest lesson of Voelker's legacy: Go, young man, and find it for yourself. ∽

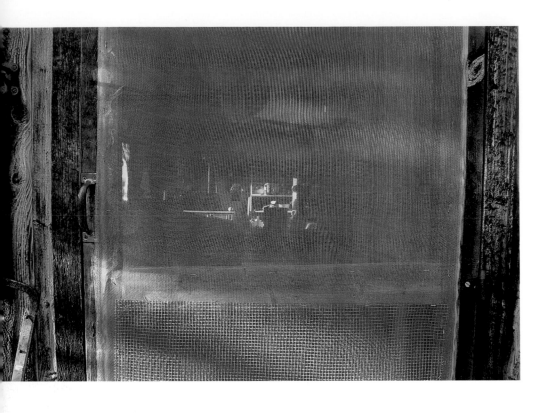

Fishing, Wishing, and Watching

My father and the judge made conversation by the cabin while I walked down to the water where a small dock protruded from thick bramble bushes that lined the entire rim of the pond. I stepped out to the end and squatting down, was struck by the illusion of depth created by auburn water, rich with tannin, over black silt. From farther back it could have been 10 or 20 feet deep, but up close, at most, the water looked only three or four and most of it appeared to be a foot or less. I stuck a stick into the bottom, and it disappeared into the silt without hitting firm ground. Then I stood up, and for some time watched the long draw of upstream water while the men chatted and unpacked gear. I did not see rising trout and I felt poorly about my prospects. Still, I was moved to be in so remote and rugged a landscape, the guest of a famous, gracious man who placed fishing above all things, and I remember a calm comfort, gratitude, and a sense of belonging that would one day call me back.

To my left, downstream, a trail led through tall hemlocks and pines over moss-covered bedrock to the narrow neck of the hourglass pond where a wooden bridge spanned the creek, complete with church pews, one facing upstream, the other down, and staggered, so that fishermen sitting across from each other could watch the water and not each other. Here, he had said, was a place for "trout devotionals." A wrought-iron weather vane shaped like a fish was raised like a steeple between the pews. I peered over the side, hoping to spot a fish or two, but didn't, and so sat down while a family of chipmunks skittered to my feet with brazen expectation, having been fed there so frequently.

*Milk crates were used
for casting stations.*

"Well," my father called to me through the pines, "You fishing?" I hopped up and hiked back to the Scout, rigged up my rod and strapped into my oversized rubber waders.

"I'll take the lad," the judge said, dutifully. Following him over the bridge, I then stumbled behind his steady gait along planks that spanned unevenly the muck and grassy ground to a casting station made of wooden crates about midway up the main pond. My father watched us from the dock with a camera.

"Be my guest, my boy," the Judge said with a swagger and a wave toward the pond.

I was an adequate fisherman on rivers with wet flies because I knew how to present a muddler minnow downstream—a skill that did not necessarily require casting. I'd learned I could take a handful of line and pitch it upstream above a pool, letting it sink, then mend line like crazy into the current, getting a streamer deep down and across until I thought it would be in front of a decent fish—then I'd quickly strip it across the pool. It was ugly but effective.

Here, though, on Frenchman's with the Master at my side, I felt whoozie, knowing I had nothing in my bag of tricks to help me. But I tried.

First, with eyes focused on the water I stripped line out of my reel straight into the brambles, snagging up a rat's nest before I could even begin a cast. Apologizing, I cleared the knots, holding excess line in my left hand. Now focusing again on a dark spot of water 20 feet out, I set myself like a quarterback, released the slack line in my hand and whipped a back cast up high into the one shrub behind us, violating the first rule of the forward cast, which is first to check on the back cast.

Now I was breathing embarrassment, defeat and shame, hobbling through the brush to free my fly from top branches, only to discover my line had been dragging behind me all the way, tangling like silly string in the brambles.

*An infamous trout rise
on Voelker's Pond.*

I struggled back to him, finally reassembled, and he looked down at me with a wry smile. "You might want to work on the roll cast, my boy," he said, and stepped up, stripping line from his reel and singing it once through the guides of his old cane rod into the pond. Then, with a slow back and upward motion he lifted the line briefly toward himself and slightly off the water until it bowed just behind the rod tip, and in one fluid motion he put on forward pressure, accelerating the line into a loop, lifting the entire length of line, leader, tippet and fly with a graceful flip, 15 feet out, then again, looping line nearly halfway across the pond. I thought of an old sailor I'd seen in Harbor Springs who tied a bowline one-handed, with a single flip of the arm, a trick I never mastered, or a crusty

old cowboy who could loop your boot while riding, whistling "Dixie" too. Within three casts he was landing a trout.

He released the troutling and stepped aside, smiled, then wandered up to another station while I set about trying to imitate his fluid motions by piling line into the water, no doubt terrorizing trout for a full half hour, until at last I caught my shirtsleeve, then nearly pierced my nose with a number four Muddler Minnow. With that I decided nonchalantly to excuse myself, hobbling back to the bridge where I settled in, feeding the chipmunks and watching the judge roll out his line.

My father had been out of sight downstream at the large beaver dam all morning. Just after midday he met me on the bridge and claimed to have caught a few small trout that he released, but nothing more. I described my roll-casting fiasco, and he sat with me for awhile, then he headed toward the truck to get out of his waders.

Watching the judge fish, I thought in my juvenile way that he might have offered me more instruction. But that was the way of these men, to show me once or twice and leave me alone to face my inadequacies and inaccuracies. Failure is good. It teaches.

I'm not sure how much it mattered to them if I persevered in this or other matters. In fishing, as in life, I would be learning alone how to be rejected, to fail and fail again, so that in the end, whether intended or not, I might discover a proper perspective, a set of priorities, and here anyway, let the landscape be the teacher.

And so, Frenchman's teaches that joy is in the pursuit as much as the catching, or you'll find certain misery much of the time; joy is in the *opportunity*, so that you'll not forget gratitude; and in the failures, since we learn the same lessons over and over—how to observe, to approach, to find fluidity of movement that communicates with the living world.

Still, I wished I'd caught a fish. ∼

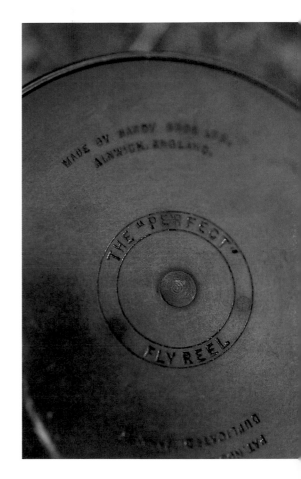

"There is no substitute for fishing sense, and if a man doesn't have it, verily, he may cast like an angel and still use his creel largely to transport sandwiches and beer." – J.V.

54

Cocktails and Cribbage with the Men

That day, sitting on the bridge watching him, I didn't know who he was, not really. I understood he was an important man, but I hadn't read his books yet. Still, something struck me deeply about him. I never got to know my own grandfather, but while writing this book I found from my mother that the judge and he had a grand old time one summer night in my backyard, drinking together into the wee hours. My mother was a good friend to Voelker's wife, Grace, and I wondered what the women endured with these men.

But that day, after an hour or so, his casts could not evoke another rise, so he ambled back to me at the bridge and sat down. I could not think of a thing to say, so we sat for a few minutes of silence on the pews. My father soon joined us and we all sat silently for some time suspended over the glassy pond, the wilderness on one side, the cabin on the other.

Then at once, we all breathed out loud, stood up and shuffled over to the cabin. There were sandwiches and sodas for me in the cooler outside, but like a boy at a tavern door with a message for his father, I did not know whether I was welcome to enter, and neither man seemed interested in me. The two had already made sandwiches and the judge mixed up his legendary old-fashioneds in tin cups.

"Well, sir," I heard the judge say, "would you like a friendly wager and a chance at the title?"

*A John Voelker favorite—
an "old-fashioned."*

Serious men deep in competition do not typically request the company of long-haired fifteen year olds, but having nowhere else to go, I crept into the cabin with the notion that perhaps I'd be included. Neither man suggested I leave, so I watched my father somehow win the first round of cribbage, relieving the judge of a prized quarter, handed over to him by a much surprised and dissatisfied Upper Peninsula Cribbage Champion, who in turn suggested another game and another wager, five dollars. A friendly tension even a vacant teenager could detect suddenly seeped through the cabin, making it seem much smaller, so not comprehending cribbage or half their witticisms and allusions anyway, I slipped outside and walked up on the high bank overlooking the pond, sitting by myself for a long time, thinking. Later, my father would tell me the old man skunked him twice in a row, taking ten bucks with a grin and an "I thank you, sir."

By then, the day was spent, the fishing was over and we followed the judge out, somehow arriving on pavement in a manner of minutes, when it had taken hours on the way in. ～

On His Justice's Flies

I'm forty-one with few vices left, and I envy no one. I do, however, covet other men's fly collections, when they surpass my own.

It is a weakness compounded by my own compulsion to give away the flies I've spent the winter tying, to friends, even to strangers at times, just for the simple joy of believing their fishing will be improved by my inventions. So imagine my eyes when Voelker's grandson, Adam, first unveiled the vast array of flies he'd inherited: piles of them, a veritable history lesson in the evolution of the fly from the 1930s to the present, mostly tied by Voelker's friends— and none tied by Voelker himself. "Far from being able to tie a fly, I am barely able to unzip one," he wrote.

Adam had stepped to a closet in his living room and handled a large crate, unpacking box after box, some handmade out of plastic pill containers and such, as I recall the Judge having when I first met him (he had a box on which he'd written: "WARNING: This box contains the world's deadliest flies"), some in pricey Wheatley boxes (most of which, Adam told me, were gifts), most of them curiously unorganized on the insides. Dry flies were mixed with wet, large and small, duns, emergers, streamers, no-hackles, bushy hackles in every color and combination, some elegant, some sloppy, some clearly having caught their share of fish. I picked through them, speechless.

John's favorite flies, just as he left them.

Then Adam said, "Oh," and stood up, stepping back to the closet, returning with his grandfather's vest and pulling out something silvery cupped in his hand. He set it on the counter: an old 1960s film container, tin, with a screw-on lid, dented and scuffed. He unscrewed the top and spilled out about two dozen flies: mini-streamers and size 28 midge and larvae flies. With a pencil tip, he pushed the tiniest of them aside. "This one," he said, pointing to a yellow dot on a wire hook smaller than a pencil tip, "is supposed to be the egg sack off a henspinner." He paused a moment, then said, "These were in my grandfather's breast pocket when he died." ∾

"If you are hardy enough, smoke Italian cigars. They smell like burning peat bog mixed with smoldering Bermuda onions but they're the best damned unlabeled DDT on the market; all mosquitoes in the same township immediately shrivel and zoom to earth. {Fellow fishermen occasionally follow suit.}" – J.V.

Gizmos in the Pursuit

In the cases of John Voelker and his friends, *Trout Madness* was the mother of invention. The brook trout in his pond and adjacent waterways eluded them so frequently, they set their minds constantly on ways to improve their pursuits, including building casting stations and boardwalks, but also inventing what we now find in pricey catalogs as "float tubes." Theirs were tractor inner tubes with hand-tied diaper slings that would let a man drift over water too deep for waders.

And in the case of the infamous Dancing Fly, if we are to take the story seriously, his friends learned to stand on opposite banks of the pond with their lines tied together and a fly on a dropper between them, pulling it back and forth to make it dance. And though they had a mind to do it, they fell short of fishing from balloons.

But there were other tricks. For quick extraction from one fishing hole and insertion in the next, rather than breaking down all the equipment and having to re-rig it at the next site on the river, the judge would break the rod down only, with the line and fly still rigged, laying it carefully on a towel, rolling it up and

wrapping it with pipe cleaners. That way when he arrived, it was a matter of seconds and he was on the river, fly already attached.

But to me, because of its novelty, one of the niftiest inventions was sitting on the table when Adam showed us his grandfather's deep collection of flies. There was first a homemade clip-on magnifying glass that had a Paul Young clipper and tweezer, but the novelty was this odd looking wooden clothespin with a spring on it, an item Adam thinks his grandfather may have invented himself.

It was a tool, I was told, for tying the essential but difficult knot, the "blood knot," used when a fisherman needs to link two uneven sizes of tippet or leader together. It's a painful knot to learn, requiring the tier first to hold the two unequal ends of leader together in an "X"—the thicker leader that is already attached to the line, and the new, thinner, leader or tippet he hopes to attach. He must then take one end at a time—in this case, the thinner line—twisting it four or five times around the thicker line and bringing it back to the original point of contact and through where the two pieces met originally to form the "X." He must hold it there without losing his grip as he then turns the thicker end an equal number of times over the thinner line, using one hand, since the other is busy, bringing that end back so that now both ends have passed through the hole that was formed once the second line began twisting. Most of the time failure occurs at this point, when one or both of the ends slip out and the whole mess untangles. When tied successfully, however, the knot is super strong and can be clipped smooth, so if by accident the fisherman casts poorly, the hook does not hang on his own leader.

So here is what the good judge figured out. He took a common clothespin and fit a flat piece of metal he'd designed under one of the forward pin springs so it was locked down in front, with a piece like a tail pointing toward the back of the clothespin. This tail was thin enough to slide inside a small tight spring. He inserted the spring, then locked it down near the pincher end of the clothespin using wood putty. After the putty dried, he rolled up a piece of scratch paper, sticking it under the spring, so the spring arced, opening up its coils slightly.

Now, when it came time to tie a blood knot, he could place his rod on his lap and clip the clothespin to his rod, then lay each piece of leader and tippet into the grooves of the spring. The spring held them nicely parallel and snugly so both his hands were free. He could then tie each half of the knot without ever worrying about letting go or it slipping out of his hands. He'd snug up the wraps, give a little pull on the leader and tippet, and both would pop out of the spring; the knot would tighten and be ready for trimming.

I wish I could have seen him whip up a knot like that beside some other poor sap trying to do the same, a twinkle in his eye, even if that poor sap had been me. ～

An old, reliable "Orvis" reel
from John's collection.

"I have known many fisherman but never have
I known one who could make trout feed when
they don't want to." – J.V.

"To paraphrase a deceased patriot, I regret that I have but one life to give to my fly-fishing." – J.V.

From the days when
canteens were used widely.

Dozens of polygala flowers adorn
the shoreline of the pond.

Equipment

According to Adam, after his grandfather passed away, some time went by before he could get back to Ishpeming, but when he did he discovered much of the fishing gear he would eventually inherit spread out throughout the house. In one room he found several of his grandfather's rods in a corner loosely bundled in a large wicker basket. About four or five of them were fully assembled, others not, among them, some of his grandfather's favorites. Two rods were hanging crisscrossed above the mirror in the bedroom. In the basement he found a number of empty rod tubes, some corresponding with rods upstairs, some not, most of them with lost caps and others containing extra tips but no matching rods. Reels and line and miscellaneous tools that had not been gifted away were mostly boxed up. His grandmother had neatened up most of his flies and placed them in a large cardboard box. There was no way to take an inventory. Before Adam was able to take possession of the collection, there may have been a bit of a grab bag going on among visitors, but who could say.

Of course Adam had inherited a gold mine of memorabilia, one that would arouse his interest in cane rods, their histories and restoration, and that would lead him to become a collector, connoisseur, and an authority on the evolution of American cane rods.

Of course, his grandfather knew a fine piece of split bamboo from a buggy whip. Most of the rods Adam inherited were hand built by the best craftsmen of the day and had become as much a part of the lore of his grandfather's yarns as the pond and his beloved fish car.

I sat with Adam in his kitchen, looking over the craftsmanship of a genuine Thomas rod built in 1928. It came with two tips personally restored by the legendary Paul Young in 1945.

*A collection
of Kushner, Carlson
and Thomas rods.*

This was the same rod mentioned in *Trout Magic*, where Voelker writes, "I still have several rods made by Paul [Young] himself (now prized collectors' items) including one real oldie Paul used himself, a weepy old Thomas that used to make me feel like Nijinsky himself when I get waving it with a full head of line."

Next to this rod, Adam had set out a Kushner rod, the very Kushner in the essay, "Morris the Rod Maker." Next to that, another Paul Young designed to be fished on the Au Sable from one of the classic, narrow, flat-bottomed Au Sable River boats. It's a long, beefy rod with a special thumb impression, to give power through the butt of the rod rather than the mid-section, allowing a more comfortable cast from a sitting position. For those who have a copy of *Anatomy of a Fisherman*, you can see this rod resting against a tree if you look closely at the shot of Voelker sitting in the rain. Other rods were dispersed to friends before his death, and one, an Orvis Limestone Special, along with a favorite sweater and an old tin cup, rests in the care of the Fly Fishing Hall of Fame.

Through the 1980s and '90s the technology of fly rod design blossomed, and occasionally, especially when fishing the big water on the Escanaba or when he encountered a blustery day, Voelker would set aside his willowy cane rods and pull out a meatier fiberglass model, or one particular graphite rod built in the 1970s. They were powerful tools, no doubt, but he claimed, unlike his old bamboo, they did not have "soul." Toward the end, as his powers waned, the judge was seen on Frenchman's with his favorite cane rods, rolling out fine tippets and flies, more often sitting down on a crate or a chair than standing.

Ever since hearing these stories, one question has remained with me, mostly because it reminded of my own equipment foibles. Why did the judge, knowing the value of his equipment, treat it all so nonchalantly, leaving them in corners still assembled when they should have been broken down; sticking flies in the cork butts rather than on hook eyes; losing caps to rod cases and misplacing matching parts?

Perhaps it was a sentiment, or rather, an accident of personality I may share with him. He no doubt appreciated a lovely rod—as do I—especially those handcrafted beauties offered to him by friends. But I think it's clear that to a man in love with the woods, rods, reels, flies— they are only tools—beautiful tools, no doubt, but only tools.

Nowhere in his Testament of a Fisherman, his most compressed and often quoted expression on fishing, does he mention the sensuous feel of a rod or reel, the elegance of a perfect cast, or the power a well-made rod can wave. He never mentions the clocklike precision or capacities or the thrill of line whining out of a

Hardy reel at the behest of a granddaddy trout. These may have all been sweet possessions and sweet pleasures, but they had nothing to do with love. "I fish because I love to," he said. He loved the trout and the environs where they are found. He loved the peace and solitude these environs offered him. Equipment—rods, reels, lines, tippets, and flies—they were only possessions—coveted no doubt by some men—brandished with pride by others—but to him, I think they were merely a means for communicating with the environs he loved, and for that, in the end, no tools are necessary. And I think above all, he most loved the blessed *opportunity* to fish, and if not to fish, to sit on a church pew in the presence of water—these things above all the baubles men worship in this world.

"Only when I can no longer cast to one of my beauties will I consider letting go," he said. And though now he is gone, he leaves this lesson for those who are listening. ∿

One of John's well-kept Hardy reels.

81

"*The elusive trout at Frenchman's all seem to arrive in their watery world sporting framed master's degrees in evasion.*" – J.V.

"Alas, I've tried and I've sighed and all but cried, but I simply can't seem to tie a decent fly. Apparently I fell on my head when I was a baby or something. All my flies come out like old feather dusters." – J.V.

A Witness to the Dancing Fly

In the waning hours of the afternoon I wandered upstream on the cabin side of the pond along Voelker's trail, now moss-covered and lush, but still imprinted in the soft earth. It is always cooler under the hemlocks and cedars, shaded and fragrant. Past the second dam the trail faded, overgrown with lush foliage, swamp grasses and thistles, wildflowers and lichens. Dense, mature hemlocks and cedars lined the second pond on the cabin side where the bank falls steeply to the water, but on the far side drowned hardwoods lined the shore, some of them having toppled into the water, others hollowed out over the years, their trunks pocked by woodpeckers.

The last fishable pond upstream was like this. Half submerged maples and aspens lay one over another, providing ample cover for wary trout as well as wood ducks, and good hunting for herons, raccoons, and otters, and making for tricky fishing, their branches both above and below the surface waiting to snatch a fly. Certainly the largest trout lurked far back in the deepest cover, where even a wizard could not cast a line.

It had been a rare and sensuous afternoon in the middle of May, a day devoid of human sounds, windless and warm, easing into evening. A hatch was inevitable, tangible and anticipated in the scented, humid air. By the beginnings of twilight flycatchers and cedar waxwings appeared in the treetops, now and again flipping out from branches to snatch last night's mayflies as they began their airborne mating dance. The day waned into magic time—that window of light when day creatures retreat to night, and night creatures stir to day, and the pond comes alive.

A favorite sits on top of Voelker's fly vial.

The sun passed over the tree line, casting the pond in pastel half-light while slowly, like an orchestra tuning, a chorus of crickets and cicadas and songbirds, whippoorwills and white-throated sparrows, spring peepers, crows, chickadees and jays swelled to a crescendo. Overhead a hawk circled, and a mink darted across a log into the opposite bank. Then a hatch of tiny caddis and midges and moths came on and the pond slowly percolated with feeding fish. A doe walked the shore across the way, unaware, followed by two fawns, and a great horned owl, its enormous wingspan startling me, swept up onto the top of a hollow tree, and coyotes, yip-yip-yowled and barked into the dark. A grouse drummed in the distance and woodcock made their twittering mating flights overhead. And I was glad to the brink of tears, fallen into a separate, timeless state, so much so that the pond and all its inhabitants breathed a chorus with me that I felt in the belly, in the chest. It settles from the mind to the body, to the actions of the extremities—legs sliding through water, arms testing the length of the cast, then committing, reaching up and across a log or a slow, swirling current, a quick midair mend of line, all unconscious, muscular, free. Immersed in sensuous water, giving flight and direction to the proper length of line, compensating here for breeze and there for the high cedar behind me.

Then just before full dark, there emerged from the water a rich and magical hatch of the "dancing fly" Voelker describes in *Trout Magic*, an iridescent yellow insect he aptly described as an "animated ball of fur," miniscule, and impossible to match with a fly—so far—because it literally hops on the water, stirring the fish into a frenzy and bringing the pond to a boil. I watched, absorbed, unable to catch another fish but thrilled and finally exhausted as darkness came on, the pond settled down, and I turned to the stars and sighed. ∽

"Fly-fishing for wild trout on quiet waters must be one of the toughest and craziest ways to catch fish ever invented by man, as well as among the most frustrating and humiliating." – J.V.

Native Trout and Television

In his essay, "Size Is Not the Measure," Voelker noted a growing preference fisherman were expressing for larger species of fish, claiming that he had not seen a single photo of a brook trout adorning the pages of outdoor magazines in months, maybe years, and feared that the new obsession with bigger and bigger fish was "inevitably transplanting to our trout waters the whole competitive, strident, screechingly acquisitive world of business." "Worse yet," he said, "fishermen were sacrificing one of the main rewards and solaces of going fishing at all, namely, that fishing is…the world's only sport that it is fun even to fail at." He finally admitted he was "sad beyond words that fishermen themselves would let one of the world's oldest and loveliest contemplative pastimes turn into a competitive rat race."

The judge wrote this in 1974, judiciously.

Last month, hoping to take a nap, I flipped on an outdoor channel only to see a "fly-fishing competition," in which "professional" fly-fishermen and women drew sections of a Western creek, were given time limits and set out to catch the largest possible fish for prize money, catching, measuring, and tossing back. I couldn't believe what I was watching, except that once again men have proved that anything sacred can be appropriated and packaged.

95

An old measuring stick for
those big brook trout.

Only one competitor, a woman, seemed to have a decent attitude throughout, enjoying herself, coming in third or fourth, but having had fun. For the rest, it was testosterone and intensity. After the awards, the camera lit for awhile on a pudgy young man who'd not "won" anything, holding his head in his hands to hide his tears.

I had to laugh because I couldn't reach inside the television and bop the heartsick boy upside the head. Then I sighed and thought how grounding it is to retreat to the pond, where I had inherited the priorities of a wise man, and where the world operates on principles of beauty and where every trout is a gem, not a measurement; where each is cherished for its wildness, and where we take time to note the striking variety of their complexions and color, some of them far lighter and greener, with brighter yellow spotting, while others are nearly all the deepest blue, with haloed, azure rings around radiant maroon moons intermittently spaced along their medial lines. And we notice, as fall approaches, the spawning season, their colors intensify; the larger males taking on orange bellies and hooking jaws, the blues and greens, purples and yellows, white pectoral fins and black lines. I am always amazed that these creatures—so radiant in my hand—can disappear so easily once they slip back underwater. They rival in beauty any fish in the world, freshwater or tropical.

Brown trout, and lake run rainbows no doubt, are the giants of the larger streams, and are thrilling to catch, but they are not native to Traver Country. Only the wild brook trout are indigenous here.

And in this way, they are not only great fun to pursue and fail to catch, but they represent all true inhabitants of the region—inhabitants— not immigrants or residents—but inhabitants whose lives are intertwined with every element of the landscape, the pond in which they live, its temperatures and depths. And they remind us of the other human inhabitants, like Voelker himself, a resident who stayed in his community, who witnessed its changes, heard the old dialects slowly lost to what he called a "bastard form of televese" and the influx of fast food and mass markets and strip malls and a pace of life that has led even fly fishermen to forget that every day is a glorious opportunity, and that there are no bad days on a stream.

No brook trout would have been large enough to win that competition on television. I wonder what the old judge would have said to the fisherman who wept for money and esteem on the banks of that lovely stretch of trout-rich water. ◠

"*Trout should be eaten not later than twenty-four hours after they are caught, else one might better eat damp swamp hay crowned with chain-store mustard.*" – J.V.

101

One of the many sunken docks
along the pond's edge.

Changes and Permanence

It is a harsh landscape by the pond, come winter, when on average 129 inches of snow will fall. What can creatures eat enduring an ice field like that? And consider the immigrants, also, who made their homesteads there in the 1800s, as did Voelker's family and those in the communities he knew so well.

And as a case in point from the animal world, consider that every county in the Lower Peninsula, and nearly every county in the state has had perennial overpopulations of deer except Baraga and Marquette counties and the few others on the northern rim by Lake Superior where the landscape resembles the region around the pond. And from those counties nearly all the deer that summer there migrate south in the fall by long-established routes, knowing not to return until spring.

So, in the years that have passed since John Voelker left us, approximately 1,550 inches of snow and Lord knows how much rain has fallen on the fish camp, taking with them the old bridge and pews, toppling into the pond. From a rock ledge above, when the light is right you can see the sunken structure; it has made good fish cover. Several beauties have been landed there. There is some poetic justice.

The old planks that made the boardwalks across the bog have disappeared completely, while casting stations and milk crates, all lichen and moss-covered, have drooped into the boggy ground or slipped half into the pond or rusted or disappeared altogether, so that looking at what remains one can't be sure if the weight of winter snowfall flattened them or some subterranean forces sucked them down.

The closer we look, the more respect we have for the tenacity of every living thing in and on and around the pond. A violent windstorm boasting gales of 80 mph+ hit the area around the pond this past summer, leveling trees for miles, snapping pines in half like toothpicks, knocking power and water out for people in the nearby townships, and on the pond, nearly crushing the cabin. A 40-foot hemlock fell over the road, straight for the cabin, but caught on the two larger hemlocks beside it, and on the other side large hemlocks were blown over, uprooted completely, but fell away from the cabin, uphill.

And as a testament even to the tenacity of tree life itself, across the narrows where the bridge once stood, a 40-foot hemlock had been uprooted in the storm, leaving beneath it a barren rock face. Though in the end it fell, for 30 years or more, however old it was, it had clung to the face of a billion year old, barren rock and sapped enough nutrients to grow, who knows how. When it fell, all that remained was a sheer face of granite falling straight into the pond.

Anyway, despite the clear-cuttings that have crept closer and closer, and despite whippings by Lake Superior gales, despite summer droughts and blizzards and the heavy swelling waters of spring, the pond remains the same, in shape and size and personality—enigmatic and permanent.

Not long ago, Adam gave me a first edition of *Anatomy of a Fisherman*, the photo-essay hardcover, but my wife, Lisa, had not seen it until recently. In it are several shots of Voelker on his pond, standing exactly as I have, landing one of his largest brookies of that summer in the lower pond, exactly where I stood, landing one of the largest of this summer, my wife Lisa standing by me, camera in hand.

It is uncanny...this pond, this legacy. ∾

An ancient beaver cutting near the water's edge.

A membership card from the
Michigan North Woods Club.

Old advertisements for Traver's
book, Danny and the Boys.

A View into the Upper Ponds

It was late August. A whisper of autumn had passed in the morning air, but now afternoon turned lovely, hot and blue- bright, and the mermaids sought the comforts of cover in the lower ponds, turning up their noses at every cast, no matter how delicately proposed, and no matter what elegant or gaudy fashion of fly landed at their window. Rejected, lulled a bit with conversation, I paddled upstream along the tangled shoreline, hoping at least to spot a brookie darting to or from a lair where we might visit later, but no. Instead, we hauled the canoe over the first beaver dam, a short but sturdy wall of dirt and timbers that held back the water on two sides of a small island, then paddled toward the uppermost ponds to explore. There, a series of three more dams stair-step, each above each, shallower, more tangled and narrower as they go. About a half mile up, the ponds narrow to nothing more than a tangle of blown down trees and bramble bushes beside tall cedars that canopy a cool stream of water the width of an average boy's broad jump.

We hefted the canoe over the first dam and paddled around a short bend into a wide shallow, shaped like a large teardrop, too shallow to hold fish and barely deep enough for us to make way, its bottom lush with luminous, almost fluorescent waves of feathered algae, like angel hair, mermaid hair, growing only inches under the surface but spread across the entire pond, like nothing I'd seen before. We were luxuriant in our pace, abandoning the fly rod and sauntering so we might observe, barely making way in its slight current, and noting how distinct this pond was from the deeper, more silt-bottomed pools below. In time, we slid up the right side to the top of the pool along the only submerged log in the current, scattering about a half dozen fingerling trout, then nosed the canoe into the backside of the third dam, an ancient dam, so old the bottom four feet of timbers set there by beavers generations earlier had decayed into dirt, making a solid earth embankment four feet tall.

The deepest water is often on the upstream side of dams like this where often the largest fish will hold. It is sometimes possible to stand behind the dam, your profile below the trout's window of view, and cast stealthily up and over the dam. So before hauling the canoe up, we peeked over, only to find the surface covered with a musty green-brown algae floating on the surface, backed up for 15 feet or more, looking like a warm, week-old head on a heavy malt beer. So we pulled the canoe over and paddled up past the floaties, forgetting fishing altogether, finding instead a kind of freshwater kelp rising up from the bottom, a species I'd never seen. Dense stalks, about the diameter of a quarter

and no more than a few inches apart, they clogged the entire right side of the pool and seemed to be the source of the musty algae we'd paddled through. On the left, and further ahead, storm-tossed trees uprooted by an intense summer storm had all been slammed over, parallel, side by side, their entangled limbs forming a gauntlet for the canoe and rendering the pond nearly impossible to fish with dry flies. But I noticed deep holes where the roots had been torn up, and directed a few long rejected casts at the bases of these stumps as we crept forward. Then we both stopped, staring into the water.

Below us, at the bottom of the pond, an inexplicably beautiful and chilling life form—an algae—eye at the bottom of the pond—rusty orange and strangely gelatinous at the center, then fibrous and fluorescent around the edges, surrounded by, and as if communicating with the same luminous, feathery green algae we'd seen in the lower dam. Our reflections and that of the terrestrial world wavered on the surface. We stared a long time, almost afraid to poke it with a paddle, not want to break the spell of its presence there, grinning at each other and speechless—witnesses to the secret, silent life of this watery cosmos.

Afterward, we pulled ashore finding grey, green, and bright red and amber lichens and mosses and fungi, all clinging to bare rock faces and to tree limbs and trunks, cushioning our footsteps over billion year old bedrock. The largest, clumped like cauliflower, I read later were over 50 years old, clinging tenaciously through the ravages of winter so it might emerge and thrive before our eyes.

117

Since boyhood I've canoed and waded and swum and submerged myself in lakes and ponds and rivers day and night, naked and clothed, open-eyed and masked with fins and snorkels; I've prodded and peered into currents, even crept up to undercut banks to stroke long, secretive underbellies of trout, and caught fish with my bare hands. I've emerged leech-bitten and gasped once as a snapping turtle swam between my legs. My flies have accidentally caught bats and dragonflies, a two-foot water snake and a twenty-pound carp, its scales the size of quarters and a kind of ancient shelf-fungus on its sides; I've been tormented by every kind of biting bug and the sudden smack of beaver tails at night like watermelons dropped from five-story buildings, and raccoons fighting in the black canopy above my head and wild turkey squawking into flight. I've dipped nets and cast lines and held voracious pike and helpless trout and seen the struggling eyes of animals whose lives remain as much a mystery to me as the deepest realms of space. So when Ed turned his macro-lens on the delicate, luscious and mutable hues of the brook trout from Voelker's pond, and again, onto the inexplicable algae in the upper ponds, I could not help compare the billion-dollar images the Hubble telescope retrieved from the darkest points of deep space, a focal point "the size of a grain of salt at arm's length." There, scientists discovered a million or more galaxies—*galaxies*—each as large and larger than our own....

That evening, as the sun lit the mirrored pond ablaze, I gazed along the length of water, a stranger to the secret life beneath its surface. Then, like a truce, I let the questions be, and simply, silently, worshipped. ⌁

"Most fishermen swiftly learn that it's a pretty good rule never to show a favorite spot to any fisherman you wouldn't trust with your wife." – J.V.

Voelker's grandson ties
into a nice one.

*A beautiful look at
a brook trout before
its release.*

A Season's Send-Off

A week before, Indian summer kept temperatures in the '70s, and by afternoon enough grasshoppers, beetles, and other winged terrestrials hazarded into the water to stir up some good fishing. There had even been a sudden burst of feeding at dusk, tailing off at dark when we paddled in for the night.

But now the last day of the season had arrived and the night before, the first serious forces of autumn swooped down from Canada in a single blow that meteorologists might call an "Alberta Clipper," but locals are more likely to call a "Canadian Crap Hammer." Gale force winds led a lightning-blazed, mop-bucket downpour, passing over the peninsula like a cold angry hand, wiping away the warmth of Indian summer for good. Then overnight a hard, frosty stillness iced the windows of our cars and the clouds blew off, chilling the temperature down in the morning and killing off insect activity and trout feeding all day.

Perhaps it's because the pond's springs seep up from aquifers so cold and deep the weather we fishermen use to predict the fishing is virtually irrelevant to the creatures below. Or perhaps it's because the fish food in Voelker's pond takes mostly subsurface forms and follows cryptic codes of conduct we'll never fully decipher. No matter, it's clear the pond, like any fascinating, complicated personality, shows us only what it wants to, the face that meets the faces. After a lifetime on the pond Voelker himself could not explain its moods beyond the fact that the pond has a mind of its own and can be wooed only when it wishes to be. These thoughts were with us that late September evening, when the pond offered only a silent, blank stare with dark coming on fast.

125

But it is the pond's notorious moodiness that, ironically, can inspire hope, because it may decide at any time to break all rules of engagement, and offer up a lovely trout at the damnedest time, under the goofiest conditions. Or not.

Still, though a fisherman might not recognize (or even *see*) the insects the trout feed on, from May through August he can pretty much anticipate morning hatches to be followed by terrestrial activity in the afternoon, and occasional evening hatches, after which the pond shuts down for the night so fishermen can stare at the stars or sit around the campfire smoking cigars and reading selections from *Danny and the Boys* and *Trout Magic* out loud, laughing until they wet themselves.

But I'd never bothered fishing the pond at night—having never heard a rise after dark—and because it's common knowledge that brook trout hide out at night. At least this is true of most brook trout on most streams in the Lower Peninsula—where they have an understandable reason. First, Lower Peninsula brookies tend to be small—averaging six or seven inches. Others may claim more success than I, but I'm giddy when I release 10-inchers and overjoyed with 12- and 13-inchers (this summer I about fell over in glory when I landed and released a 15-incher). The difference is, below the Mackinac bridge, most brook trout have to share the water with brown trout, a species that in deeper rivers can grow over 20 and up to 30 inches long. Once matured like this, browns tend to hide all day and then prowl the streams at night, especially muggy nights in July and August after the mayfly hatches die down, seeking out big meals like baitfish, crayfish, even wayfaring mice—and certainly wayfaring brook trout. An eight-inch brook trout would make a nutritious hors-d'oeuvre for a mature brown.

Thus, all but perhaps the few largest brook trout hide out until dawn on rivers like these. And on Voelker's pond in my experience, nighttime meant bedtime for brookies too, even though the fish there are safe from marauding browns.

Under a moonless sky, the temperature dropping, mist came off the water now. Mist on the water and cold nights are never productive, but suddenly, a tremendous "glunk" echoed down the stream, a granddaddy rising, the largest I'd ever heard on this pond, the mythical fish Voelker claimed to have caught by accident once while competing with his friends, trying quickly to reel in a smaller trout when the big one hit.

At least he sounded upstream, perhaps in the hollow beyond the weed bed, and between the bramble-covered bank and sunken log. If only he would rise again I might locate him. So I waited. He must rise again, I thought. He will rise.

But nothing.

It was deep-hall dark, and the casting was dangerous—twigs and branches I could not see, but still I tried dragging flies, changing them three or four times and started casting blind all over until finally hooking up on the weed bed, snagged solidly. Then, unbelievably, from far below, another "glunk" echoed over the pond, of equal magnitude.

"My Lord," I whimpered, scampering to release my hook and finally snapping off the fly, fumbling for my light and tying on a new one and casting blindly again for the longest time.

"It's over," I said, at last.

We lugged the canoe up and strapped it down on the car, cleaned up camp, put the paddles and rods away, made tea and walked down to the fire.

And in the distance, echoing over the pond, "Glunk."

My jaw dropped.

"Look who gets the last word." ∽

"Fly rods are like Cornish pasties—both are best made for love rather than for money." – J.V.

Often, Voelker would choose the cork handle for setting his hook.

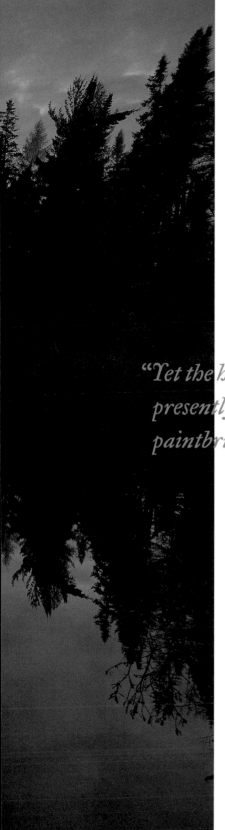

Epilogue

from Voelker's *Trout Madness*

"*Yet the hazy and glorious days glide by on golden wings, and presently here and there the leaves grow tinted by subtle fairy paintbrushes and flash their red warnings of impending fall.*"

"Even the trout become more brilliant in hue
and grow heavy and loaded with spawn."

"And then, lo, one day we tired fishermen drag ourselves abroad only to discover that the stricken summer has waned into colorful northern autumn, like a beautiful woman flushed with the fevers of approaching death."

"It is the last day of fishing; the annual hibernation is once again at hand." — J.V.

Acknowledgments

From the Author
To Dr. W.L. McCullough for taking me to meet John Voelker twenty-seven years ago, and to Mary Ann McCullough for holding down the fort while we were gone. To my wife, Lisa McCullough for her love and support throughout the project; I could not have done it without you. To my lovely daughters, Meghan and Madison, my reasons for leaving a legacy behind.

From the Photographer
With love, to my future fly-fisherman, my son Jake Wargin. Thank you for loving the outdoors as you do. With love and admiration, to my wife, Kathy-jo Wargin for her professionalism, encouragement, bravery in the face of adversity, and for her loving ways. For the steadfast professional support and encouragement we have received over the years from Mike DiCosola and Peder Nelson of Chromaticity, Inc.; Cathy Neff and Jack Zlotow from First Community Bank, thank you for treating people who build careers in the arts with respect. Thank you to Jim and Carol Kelly for always believing. To Bill and Julie Norcross, a heart-felt thanks for your support and friendship.

This book would not have been possible without the generosity and assistance of John Voelker's grandson, Adam Tsaloff and his wife Mary.

We are additionally indebted to John Voelker Overturf and to Ernest Baines "Woody" Wood, to whom we vow future bridge-building assistance, in spirit if not in actual effort.

We thank the active members of Kitchie Hill for their permission to reprint Mr. Voelker's *Testament of a Fisherman* and other passages from his work.

Specifically, we thank Julie Cohen, Elizabeth Tsaloff, and Grace Wood, and in particular, Grace Wood for saving us chicken and biscuits the day we could not stop for lunch.